21 Days
OF LOVE LETTERS
TO *Yourself*

A Guided Self-Love Journal

JNT Ventures

hello@joynicole.co

joynicole.co

PHOTOGRAPHY DONE BY Blake Jackson

To all the women in my life that helped me realize my self-worth, thank you.

To the person who is holding this journal right now, thank you. Your support means the world to me.

Intro

Have you ever treated a lover better than you treated yourself? Don't lie to me girl! I know you have! We've all done that. For years, I loved my romantic partners more than I loved myself. I was treating them in ways that I had NEVER treated myself. I wrote them beautiful words of encouragement (to which they responded "Damn, that's deep") and made grandiose gestures of love. Listen, I've even cosigned on a car before. I've done it all for the men I loved. It was draining. I was looking for their approval. I was looking for them to tell me that I was worthy of their love and respect. I was the ultimate "pick me". I've sucked and swallowed men who NEVER even went down on me. Girl, I didn't protect my energy AT ALL. I wanted to be loved so bad that I accepted abuse so that I wouldn't be abandoned. All of this because I didn't have a special relationship with myself.

I didn't even particularly like myself. I did everything to numb the pain. No matter how much the alcohol made me blackout and forget EVERYTHING. No matter how many times I fucked that guy. It all still hurt. It didn't go away. It didn't go away until I wanted it for myself.

Through a journey of mirror work, affirmations, and tapping I started to feel better about myself. Then, one day, out of the blue, I thought of writing really sweet love letters...to myself. I thought about all the times that I wrote beautiful love letters to men who didn't give a fuck and I always wanted one in return. So I decided I would write to myself the love letter that I always wanted. Once I started, I couldn't stop. It was so EASY and fun. I told myself things that I always wanted to hear from my lovers. I started treating myself like the lover I've always wanted because I AM the lover I've always wanted. And you are too. You are your greatest love and I know right now it seems impossible to love yourself. Maybe you just made a HUGE mistake. Or maybe your "perfect" lover left. Or maybe you just keep dealing with fuck boy after fuck boy and have never been in a "real" relationship. I'm here to tell you that NONE of those things determine your self-worth or how loveable you are. You are very loveable and hopefully, through these next three weeks, you can start on the continuous journey of self-love.

It's not a destination! You don't wake up one day and NEVER hate how your body looks. After this guided journal I cannot promise you there won't be days like that. I cannot promise you that you'll be confident enough to do whatever you want. What I will promise is that when those feelings of self-doubt creep up, you'll say "FUCK THAT! I'm a bad bitch." What I can promise is when you try on that Fashion Nova dress that you should've got in an XL instead of a large, you'll say " Fuck it, I still look really good!" I will promise that when that fuck boy doesn't text/call you back; right before you send him a long-ass paragraph text that he won't read, you'll stop and say "Thank u, next". I'm not promising anything out of the ordinary. I don't want to sell you on false dreams. I will say that the phrase "Practice makes perfect" is true. You gotta keep at this self-love, baby. The most important (and longest) relationship you'll ever have is with yourself, make it a good one.

All I really want from you is for you to improve your state of mind, have fun, and be nice to yourself! We are our own worst critics. The way we talk about ourselves we would never say that to our best friend. So as you write these love letters to yourself, I want you to remember to stay kind, stay present, and stay sweet to yourself.

To get the most out of this guided journal, I recommend including it in your morning routine. Doing this guided journal first thing in the morning will help keep your mind in a "self-love" state of being. I've included a nightly gratitude list so that every night you can write down five things you appreciated that day.

I am a

magnificent

child of the

Universe

Love Letter of Apology

First day! And hold on tight because we're about to blast off on the feels mobile (please laugh at my corny jokes, thanks!). I want you to write yourself an apology. The apology that you've been waiting for from your abusive ex, the one you never got from your parents, the apology you most desperately need to give to yourself. Tell yourself how sorry you are that you've said those horrible things. Tell yourself how remorseful you are that you let that man into your life...again and again and again. Also end all of your love letters with "I love you so much, *[insert your dope ass name here]*" After you do, I want you to read it two times from two different perspectives. Once, as the person that's receiving the apology and once, as an unbiased person who just found this letter on the street. I want you to detach after that. Cry if you need to. Perhaps tap away some of the bad shit that came up (there are a ton of guided tappings on YouTube, check my website for resources).

ACTION STEP: *Go to your bathroom mirror and say "I'm sorry, I'm so sorry. I'll take better of care of you from here on out." Say at least ten times and remember to look deep into your eyes and feel the words as you say them.*

....

....

....

....

....

....

....

....

....

....

....

....

....

....
....
....
....
....
....
....
....
....
....
....
....
....
....
....
....

How difficult was today's love letter prompt? (With 10 being the HARDEST thing EVERRR)

① ② ③ ④ ⑤ ⑥ ⑦ ⑧ ⑨ ⑩

How difficult was the action step?? (With 10 being the HARDEST thing EVERRR)

① ② ③ ④ ⑤ ⑥ ⑦ ⑧ ⑨ ⑩

Nightly Gratitude List:

1. ....
2. ....
3. ....
4. ....
5. ....

I am

divinely

guided

Love Letter of Forgiveness

Day 2, baby girl! We're on a roll. So now that you've apologized to yourself, it's time to forgive. Depending on your headspace, forgiving may be harder than the apology or vice versa. So many times, we are so quick to forgive other people in our lives for doing ATROCIOUS things to us, but we fall short on forgiving ourselves. Forgiving yourself is hard especially when you don't think you're worthy of forgiveness. Reread the letter you wrote yourself on day one and sit with it again. Read it as if your ex-lover wrote it. Read it as if your ex-best friend wrote it. Then say out loud that you love and forgive yourself. Then get to writing! You can note how painful the things you did to yourself were. Just remember to be in a state of love and forgiveness the whole time. Remember to stay soft in your forgiveness.

ACTION STEP: *Say out loud "[Insert your really cool name], I love you and forgive you with my whole heart." When you say this make sure you go to the mirror and say it to yourself. Write it down on a piece of paper. Keep the piece of paper in your wallet or on your mirror.*

....
....
....
....
....
....
....
....
....
....
....
....
....
....
....
....
....

How difficult was today's love letter prompt? (With 10 being the HARDEST thing EVERRR)

① ② ③ ④ ⑤ ⑥ ⑦ ⑧ ⑨ ⑩

How difficult was the action step?? (With 10 being the HARDEST thing EVERRR)

① ② ③ ④ ⑤ ⑥ ⑦ ⑧ ⑨ ⑩

Nightly Gratitude List:

1. ....

2. ....

3. ....

4. ....

5. ....

I am
fearfully and
wonderfully
made

Love Letter of Self-Confidence

Let's have some fun (finally!). I want you to write a letter to yourself all about the great physical features that you love about yourself. Your dazzling smile. Dat ASS. Your killer waist. Your deep brown eyes. Your cute nose. I want you to write the letter in the voice of the really drunk girl in the bathroom at your local bar. Be super duper sweet and super specific! Are you thicker than a bowl of oatmeal? Are your toes like hella suckable? Are your titties really SITTING today? TELL YO SELF. You are really a bad bitch among bad bitches. It would be really nice for you to hear that from yourself. Have fun with this prompt and really get into details. Be extra and dramatic AF.

ACTION STEP: *Take some selfies today. One of your face, one of your whole body, and one of you completely nude. And then if you're feeling really good, send them to somebody! All three of them. Someone who is really going to gas you up.*

....
....
....
....
....
....
....
....
....
....
....
....
....
....
....
....

How difficult was today's love letter prompt? (With 10 being the HARDEST thing EVERRR)

① ② ③ ④ ⑤ ⑥ ⑦ ⑧ ⑨ ⑩

How difficult was the action step?? (With 10 being the HARDEST thing EVERRR)

① ② ③ ④ ⑤ ⑥ ⑦ ⑧ ⑨ ⑩

Nightly Gratitude List:

1. ....

2. ....

3. ....

4. ....

5. ....

I am
creative

DAY 4

Perfect Imperfections

If you really want to start on this journey of loving yourself, you have to love ALL of yourself this includes things that you deem as your "flaws". Today, I want you to focus on a physical feature that you don't particularly care for. Maybe it's your stretch marks or cellulite? For me, a lot of my physical self-consciousness fell on my teeth. I'm still working on it, to be honest, but ever since, I made peace with my teeth. I smile A LOT more and without my teeth covered. So today pick a physical feature that's hard for you to look at in the mirror or in pictures. First, write a letter to that "flaw" about how sorry you are for being so mean and saying such horrible things to it. Then follow up by saying you will try your very best to be more loving towards it. Write your letter like you're speaking to a young child. Be very sweet and loving. Afterward, I want you to go in the mirror and tell that "flaw" that you love it! Tell your body that along with taking care of it that you'll also start talking way nicer to it. It would great if you include this in your morning routine so that for the rest of the day you can practice saying very nice things to your "flaw" as you pass by mirrors.

ACTION STEP: *When you come home for the day, strip naked and look at your whole body. Then tell yourself you love yourself for 20 minutes while playing your favorite songs.*

....
....
....
....
....
....
....
....
....
....
....
....

....

....

....

....

....

....

....

....

....

....

....

....

....

....

....

....

....

How difficult was today's love letter prompt? (With 10 being the HARDEST thing EVERRR)

① ② ③ ④ ⑤ ⑥ ⑦ ⑧ ⑨ ⑩

How difficult was the action step?? (With 10 being the HARDEST thing EVERRR)

① ② ③ ④ ⑤ ⑥ ⑦ ⑧ ⑨ ⑩

Nightly Gratitude List:

1. ....

2. ....

3. ....

4. ....

5. ....

I am

abundant

Love Letter of Great Friendship

How ya feeling so far?? Today, let's focus on how you're the best friend anyone can have! So I know you're like "Bitch, I'm a bad friend. I haven't texted back my friends in WEEKS. They probably kicked me out the group chat." And to that I'll say, BITCH, this is a "self-love" journal, not a "beat myself up" journal. So stop that shit. You are a great friend. Do you always give the BEST gifts? Or the best advice? Maybe you always remember your friend's birthdays. Or maybe you always volunteer as the designated driver. You don't have to wait for other people to celebrate you. Write a letter about all of the amazing things you've done as a friend. You are a really good friend and you do need to hear that as often as possible. As always use your name often and think of scenarios when you were a top-notch friend.

Aciton Step: *Call one of your closest friends and tell them what an awesome friend they are. Really go into details and let them know that you really really appreciate them.*

....

....

....

....

....

....

....

....

....

....

....

....

....

....

....

....

....

....

....

....

....

....

....

....

....

....

....

....

....

....

....

....

How difficult was today's love letter prompt? (With 10 being the HARDEST thing EVERRR)

① ② ③ ④ ⑤ ⑥ ⑦ ⑧ ⑨ ⑩

How difficult was the action step?? (With 10 being the HARDEST thing EVERRR)

① ② ③ ④ ⑤ ⑥ ⑦ ⑧ ⑨ ⑩

Nightly Gratitude List:

1. ....

2. ....

3. ....

4. ....

5. ....

I am

pure magic

Perfect Imperfections

More perfect imperfections! You are perfect just the way you are, so no more calling your physical insecurities flaws. Once again, you can choose a different perfect imperfection or the same one each time. There are no rules! Do what you know you need to do. So again write a love letter to whichever perfect imperfection you pick and feel that insecurity melt away.

ACTION STEP: *Make a self-love playlist. On Day 4, I said to play your favorite songs; well, now, I want you to make a playlist that makes you feel really good about yourself. Every song that you add on to the playlist should make you feel like you're THAT bitch.*

....
....
....
....
....
....
....
....
....
....
....
....
....
....
....
....

How difficult was today's love letter prompt? (With 10 being the HARDEST thing EVERRR)

① ② ③ ④ ⑤ ⑥ ⑦ ⑧ ⑨ ⑩

How difficult was the action step?? (With 10 being the HARDEST thing EVERRR)

① ② ③ ④ ⑤ ⑥ ⑦ ⑧ ⑨ ⑩

Nightly Gratitude List:

1. ....

2. ....

3. ....

4. ....

5. ....

I am

worthy

DAY 7

Let's talk about sex, baby! I know you're probably thinking, "What the hell does this have to do with my self-esteem and loving myself?" Baby girl, EVERYTHING. So much of our confidence (or lack thereof) shows up in our sexual performance. I want you to write a real nasty love letter to yourself. I basically want you to sext yourself. At first, it might be weird. But once you do it, BITCH, you're gonna feel like a sex goddess.Own your horniness, don't be ashamed. If you throw it back like a pro, tell yo self. If you give better sloppy toppy than Teanna Trump, compliment yourself. Those are skills hunty! Afterward, grab your vibrator and show yourself some love. Or use your hand if you're a true do it yourself type of girl. to Or use your hand if you're a true "do it yourself" type of girl. Have fun and please have an orgasm!

ACTION STEP: *At the peak of your orgasm, think about something that you really want! Is it a Jeep Wrangler or just a butt load of money? A sexy ass partner? Whatever it is, think about while you bust that nut!*

....

....

....

....

....

....

....

....

....

....

....

....

....

....

....

....

....

....

....

....

....

....

....

....

....

....

....

....

....

....

....

How difficult was today's love letter prompt? (With 10 being the HARDEST thing EVERRR)

① ② ③ ④ ⑤ ⑥ ⑦ ⑧ ⑨ ⑩

How difficult was the action step?? (With 10 being the HARDEST thing EVERRR)

① ② ③ ④ ⑤ ⑥ ⑦ ⑧ ⑨ ⑩

Nightly Gratitude List:

1. ....

2. ....

3. ....

4. ....

5. ....

I deserve

the best

Perfect Imperfections

More perfect imperfections! You are perfect just the way you are, so no more calling your physical insecurities flaws. Once again you can choose a different perfect imperfection or the same one each time. There are no rules! Do what you know you need to do. So again write a love letter to whichever perfect imperfection you pick and feel that insecurity melt away.

ACTION STEP: *Write out the names of women that you admire or aspire to be, then next to their names, write out the word that best describes them. After that, write out affirmations with all of those words. Like if you said, "Cardi B is Bold," you would write an affirmation saying, "I am bold." Get it? I like to write mine on colorful stickies and stick them all around my apartment.*

....

....

....

....

....

....

....

....

....

....

....

....

....

....

....

....

....

How difficult was today's love letter prompt? (With 10 being the HARDEST thing EVERRR)

① ② ③ ④ ⑤ ⑥ ⑦ ⑧ ⑨ ⑩

How difficult was the action step?? (With 10 being the HARDEST thing EVERRR)

① ② ③ ④ ⑤ ⑥ ⑦ ⑧ ⑨ ⑩

Nightly Gratitude List:

1. ....

2. ....

3. ....

4. ....

5. ....

I am
important

DAY 9

Love Letter of Romantic Love

It's time to talk about what a great girlfriend, wife, partner, etc you are. Think about your last romantic relationship and think of all the things that you did right. Were you attentive? Did you watch football for them? Did you throw them the best birthday party ever? Write a loving thank you note to yourself. Write as if you did all that stuff for yourself. Anyone would be lucky as fuck to be in a relationship with you. I want you to start talking to yourself like that. "...but what if I've never been in a 'real' romantic relationship before??" Now I KNOW you know what a great girlfriend you would be! You know you've thought about this more than once or twice.

ACTION STEP: *Buy yourself some flowers today. You are your greatest love! Start treating yourself like it.*

....

....

....

....

....

....

....

....

....

....

....

....

....

....

....

....

....

....

....

....

....

....

....

....

....

....

....

....

....

....

....

....

....

How difficult was today's love letter prompt? (With 10 being the HARDEST thing EVERRR)

① ② ③ ④ ⑤ ⑥ ⑦ ⑧ ⑨ ⑩

How difficult was the action step?? (With 10 being the HARDEST thing EVERRR)

① ② ③ ④ ⑤ ⑥ ⑦ ⑧ ⑨ ⑩

Nightly Gratitude List:

1. ....

2. ....

3. ....

4. ....

5. ....

I have

a purpose

DAY 10

Perfect Imperfections

More perfect imperfections! You are perfect just the way you are, so no more calling your physical insecurities flaws. Once again, you can choose a different perfect imperfection or the same one each time. There are no rules! Do what you know you need to do. So, again, write a love letter to whichever perfect imperfection you pick and feel that insecurity melt away.

ACTION STEP: *On your social media, every time you see a girl post a selfie, compliment her genuinely.*

....

....

....

....

....

....

....

....

....

....

....

....

....

....

....

....
....
....
....
....
....
....
....
....
....
....
....
....
....
....
....
....
....
....

How difficult was today's love letter prompt? (With 10 being the HARDEST thing EVERRR)

① ② ③ ④ ⑤ ⑥ ⑦ ⑧ ⑨ ⑩

How difficult was the action step?? (With 10 being the HARDEST thing EVERRR)

① ② ③ ④ ⑤ ⑥ ⑦ ⑧ ⑨ ⑩

Nightly Gratitude List:

1. ....
2. ....
3. ....
4. ....
5. ....

I am

beautiful

Love Letter of Great Accomplishment

Bitch, you did that! Write yourself a love letter, telling yourself how proud you are of YOU! Did you just buy some property? Signed that lease? Passed that final? Got that job? Kicked depression's ass and took a shower today? Whatever it is that you deem worthy of praise, gon' head and brush your shoulders off. You are incredible. I am so proud of you, but you really need to be proud of yourself, baby girl. I know you don't tell yourself often enough how proud you are of you, and I know sometimes you don't feel worthy. You are worthy, so go ahead and puff your chest out. This is the time to really brag about yourself.

ACTION STEP: *Google "blank certificates" and print out one of them, then write your name on it. You can give yourself an award for anything. For being the baddest bitch or passing that final. Whatever you like! Also, get yourself something sweet. Issa celebration!*

....
....
....
....
....
....
....
....
....
....
....
....
....
....
....
....

....

....

....

....

....

....

....

....

....

....

....

....

....

....

....

....

....

....

How difficult was today's love letter prompt? (With 10 being the HARDEST thing EVERRR)

① ② ③ ④ ⑤ ⑥ ⑦ ⑧ ⑨ ⑩

How difficult was the action step?? (With 10 being the HARDEST thing EVERRR)

① ② ③ ④ ⑤ ⑥ ⑦ ⑧ ⑨ ⑩

Nightly Gratitude List:

1. ....

2. ....

3. ....

4. ....

5. ....

I am

loved

DAY 12

Perfect Imperfections

More perfect imperfections! You are perfect just the way you are, so no more calling your physical insecurities flaws. Once again you can choose a different perfect imperfection or the same one each time. There are no rules! Do what you know you need to do. So again write a love letter to whichever perfect imperfection you pick and feel that insecurity melt away.

ACTION STEP: *Unfollow any Instagram account that makes you feel inadequate or not good enough.*

....
....
....
....
....
....
....
....
....
....
....
....
....
....
....
....

How difficult was today's love letter prompt? (With 10 being the HARDEST thing EVERRR)

① ② ③ ④ ⑤ ⑥ ⑦ ⑧ ⑨ ⑩

How difficult was the action step?? (With 10 being the HARDEST thing EVERRR)

① ② ③ ④ ⑤ ⑥ ⑦ ⑧ ⑨ ⑩

Nightly Gratitude List:

1. ....

2. ....

3. ....

4. ....

5. ....

I inspire others

Love Letter to Your Inner Child

I want you to grab a childhood photo of yourself. If you only have it on digital (like your phone), that's fine too. I want you to really look at yourself and try to remember how you felt at that exact moment you took that picture. Were you insecure? Were you sad? Were you really really happy?? I want you to write a beautiful letter to that small little being. Tell them that you love them very much and that everything is going to be ok. Compliment their insecurities. Tell them the things you wanted to hear when you were them. It's ok if this is a little tough. So much of our trauma started way before we knew what trauma was. We carry these deep wounds into our adulthood and it affects every aspect of our lives. Once you start healing your inner child, you will open up some amazing and wonderful things in your life. I promise! Start with this letter. Let's start the healing process now.

ACTION STEP: *What was your favorite thing to do as a child? Did you like coloring? Playing "make-believe"? Rollerblading? Whatever it is, today, I want you to set aside some time to do that. Let your inner child play!*

....
....
....
....
....
....
....
....
....
....
....
....
....
....
....
....
....
....

How difficult was today's love letter prompt? (With 10 being the HARDEST thing EVERRR)

① ② ③ ④ ⑤ ⑥ ⑦ ⑧ ⑨ ⑩

How difficult was the action step?? (With 10 being the HARDEST thing EVERRR)

① ② ③ ④ ⑤ ⑥ ⑦ ⑧ ⑨ ⑩

Nightly Gratitude List:

1. ....
2. ....
3. ....
4. ....
5. ....

I am
more than
good enough

Perfect Imperfections

More perfect imperfections! You are perfect just the way you are, so no more calling your physical insecurities flaws. Once again you can choose a different perfect imperfection or the same one each time. There are no rules! Do what you know you need to do. So again write a love letter to whichever perfect imperfection you pick and feel that insecurity melt away.

ACTION STEP: *Do your makeup today like you're going on your first date!*

....

....

....

....

....

....

....

....

....

....

....

....

....

....

....

....

....

How difficult was today's love letter prompt? (With 10 being the HARDEST thing EVERRR)

① ② ③ ④ ⑤ ⑥ ⑦ ⑧ ⑨ ⑩

How difficult was the action step?? (With 10 being the HARDEST thing EVERRR)

① ② ③ ④ ⑤ ⑥ ⑦ ⑧ ⑨ ⑩

Nightly Gratitude List:

1. ....

2. ....

3. ....

4. ....

5. ....

Happiness

is my

birthright

Let's talk about your personal style! I want you to love every inch of yourself, including your wardrobe. Now I know you are starting to think, "Girl, I don't even dress like how I want to because I'm too skinny, fat, I have no ass, I have hip dips, I'm not built like Instagram models.." and so on. To that I say, I DON'T CARE. You are going to find your favorite picture of yourself on Instagram (preferably one that shows your whole ensemble), and you're going to compliment those cute earrings you had on. Or those boots that no one believed were from Payless! How about that dress? Or those cute jeans? That cardigan! That lowcut top that only you could pull off. Say nice things about the way you dress now because you dress like that for a reason. You don't have to have name brand clothes and maybe you shop at Ross instead of Fashion Nova.

ACTION STEP: *Go on Pretty Little Things or whatever online fashion store you love and buy one item on there that you absolutely LOVE. You deserve it. Treat yo self.*

....
....
....
....
....
....
....
....
....
....
....
....
....
....
....
....

....
....
....
....
....
....
....
....
....
....
....
....
....
....
....
....
....

How difficult was today's love letter prompt? (With 10 being the HARDEST thing EVERRR)

① ② ③ ④ ⑤ ⑥ ⑦ ⑧ ⑨ ⑩

How difficult was the action step?? (With 10 being the HARDEST thing EVERRR)

① ② ③ ④ ⑤ ⑥ ⑦ ⑧ ⑨ ⑩

Nightly Gratitude List:

1. ....

2. ....

3. ....

4. ....

5. ....

I am

a light

in this world

Perfect Imperfections

More perfect imperfections! You are perfect just the way you are, so no more calling your physical insecurities flaws. Once again you can choose a different perfect imperfection or the same one each time. There are no rules! Do what you know you need to do. So again write a love letter to whichever perfect imperfection you pick and feel that insecurity melt away.

ACTION STEP: *Set reminders in your phone that say, "I really adore you," "I love you so much," "You are so beautiful," "You're a badass bitch," or whatever makes you feel good.*

....

....

....

....

....

....

....

....

....

....

....

....

....

....

....

....

....

....
....
....
....
....
....
....
....
....
....
....
....
....
....
....
....

How difficult was today's love letter prompt? (With 10 being the HARDEST thing EVERRR)

① ② ③ ④ ⑤ ⑥ ⑦ ⑧ ⑨ ⑩

How difficult was the action step?? (With 10 being the HARDEST thing EVERRR)

① ② ③ ④ ⑤ ⑥ ⑦ ⑧ ⑨ ⑩

Nightly Gratitude List:

1. ....
2. ....
3. ....
4. ....
5. ....

I love

my body

A Love Letter From the Future

Write another beautiful love letter to yourself, but this time I want you to write it from the future. Imagine yourself 5, 10, or even 30 years from now! I want you to tell yourself that you got this! Tell yourself about the soulmate that you manifested. Tell yourself about your thriving business. Write about how many pets you own. What's your hairdresser's name? Where do you live? Get really into it! Also, tell your present self not to worry about how all of this shit is about to happen. That is not your job yet! Your future self got it, babe. So from your future self, speak lovingly and thank yourself.

ACTION STEP: *Go to futureme.org and type out the letter you just wrote down and send it to yourself 5 years in the future. Throw some more stuff in there if you'd like and forget all about it. How cool would it be to read an email 5 years from now and see how much good shit you manifested?*

....

....

....

....

....

....

....

....

....

....

....

....

....

....

....

(lined writing space)

How difficult was today's love letter prompt? (With 10 being the HARDEST thing EVERRR)

① ② ③ ④ ⑤ ⑥ ⑦ ⑧ ⑨ ⑩

How difficult was the action step?? (With 10 being the HARDEST thing EVERRR)

① ② ③ ④ ⑤ ⑥ ⑦ ⑧ ⑨ ⑩

Nightly Gratitude List:

1. ....

2. ....

3. ....

4. ....

5. ....

I deserve

compassion

DAY 18

Perfect Imperfections

More perfect imperfections! You are perfect just the way you are, so no more calling your physical insecurities flaws. Once again you can choose a different perfect imperfection or the same one each time. There are no rules! Do what you know you need to do. So again write a love letter to whichever perfect imperfection you pick and feel that insecurity melt away.

ACTION STEP: *Take yourself on a date! If you like to go to the movies, do that. If you like fancy restaurants, go there. Treat yourself like your ideal lover would.*

....

....

....

....

....

....

....

....

....

....

....

....

....

....

....

....

How difficult was today's love letter prompt? (With 10 being the HARDEST thing EVERRR)

① ② ③ ④ ⑤ ⑥ ⑦ ⑧ ⑨ ⑩

How difficult was the action step?? (With 10 being the HARDEST thing EVERRR)

① ② ③ ④ ⑤ ⑥ ⑦ ⑧ ⑨ ⑩

Nightly Gratitude List:

1. ....

2. ....

3. ....

4. ....

5. ....

I am

intelligent

Letter from Your Higher Self/God/Universe

Let's get into our spirituality bag for a minute. I want you to write a love letter to yourself as if you were God/ Goddess/Source/Your Inner Being/The Universe, etc. I want you to tell yourself all the things you would want to hear from Your Higher Power. Tell yourself how happy you are that you were created. Tell yourself that you love you, no matter what you do or say. Speak with the confidence of an all-knowing and all-seeing Being. For example, mine would start off like, "Dear Joy, I am so glad that I made you 25 years ago. You are among one of my greatest creations and I've created galaxies that you humans have never even seen before. You are so beautiful and so precious to me. I celebrate every day you wake up. Every single day because you mean that much to me. You are forever a part of me and remember that I am always a part of you"

ACTION STEP: *If you have some sage/incense/palo santo, burn it and listen to my guided affirmation meditation that's available on my website.*

....
....
....
....
....
....
....
....
....
....
....
....

....
....
....
....
....
....
....
....
....
....
....
....
....
....
....
....
....
....

How difficult was today's love letter prompt? (With 10 being the HARDEST thing EVERRR)

① ② ③ ④ ⑤ ⑥ ⑦ ⑧ ⑨ ⑩

How difficult was the action step?? (With 10 being the HARDEST thing EVERRR)

① ② ③ ④ ⑤ ⑥ ⑦ ⑧ ⑨ ⑩

Nightly Gratitude List:

1. ....

2. ....

3. ....

4. ....

5. ....

I am

blessed

Last of Perfect Imperfections

Today is the last of perfect imperfections and I want you to be raw and real with yourself. Is it still hard for you to look at your perfect imperfection? Is it still hard to call it a "perfect" imperfection? It's ok. Be real. Self-love takes time. Social media definitely has our mind warped on how a body should look. It took more than 21 days for you to develop these insecurities and it will take more than that to conquer. You got this though. So write this letter with the same softness as before. And you don't get brownie points taken away if it's not all sunshine and rainbows.

ACTION STEP: *Write down all of your "flaws" on a piece of paper and BURN THAT SHIT. Poof! Your insecurities? Never heard of her.*

....
....
....
....
....
....
....
....
....
....
....
....
....
....
....
....

How difficult was today's love letter prompt? (With 10 being the HARDEST thing EVERRR)

① ② ③ ④ ⑤ ⑥ ⑦ ⑧ ⑨ ⑩

How difficult was the action step?? (With 10 being the HARDEST thing EVERRR)

① ② ③ ④ ⑤ ⑥ ⑦ ⑧ ⑨ ⑩

Nightly Gratitude List:

1. ....
2. ....
3. ....
4. ....
5. ....

I am
on the best path
for me

DAY 21

Wow! You finished! I'm so proud of you girl. You made the decision to love yourself more and that alone was so brave. You buying this book was an act of self-love. You are so awesome for that. So please as your last love letter to yourself, thank yourself. Really show gratitude and appreciation to you! No one made you buy this book but you. You are beginning to take such good care of yourself. The journey doesn't end here. This is only the beginning. Please come back to these love letters when your love for yourself is running on empty.

ACTION STEP: *Read all of your love letters in order and feel the love!*

....
....
....
....
....
....
....
....
....
....
....
....
....
....
....
....
....

··

··

··

··

··

··

··

··

··

··

··

··

··

··

··

··

How difficult was today's love letter prompt? (With 10 being the HARDEST thing EVERRR)

① ② ③ ④ ⑤ ⑥ ⑦ ⑧ ⑨ ⑩

How difficult was the action step?? (With 10 being the HARDEST thing EVERRR)

① ② ③ ④ ⑤ ⑥ ⑦ ⑧ ⑨ ⑩

Nightly Gratitude List:

1. ··

2. ··

3. ··

4. ··

5. ··

NOW WHAT?

Obviously the work doesn't stop here. Please remember to be gentle with your words, when speaking to yourself. Don't expect that there will be no more days of self-doubt. When those days happen, I have a whole website full of blog posts with resources on how to make those days better. You should be signed up for my mid-week pick me ups by now and those are full of self-love goodies. If you would like, please document your 21 days by using **#LoveYourSelfExtravaganzaChallenge**. Yeah, the hashtag is extra as fuck. I'm extra as fuck if you haven't noticed by now. Also, reply back to the emails that I share with you every week. Talk to me on Instagram! I'm super friendly! I mean hello, I literally call myself Friendly Neighborhood Bad Bitch (trademark pending lololol).

I love you.

Notes

Notes

Made in the USA
Middletown, DE
26 August 2022

72285115R00084